photo Man Ray, 1936

BY JAMES THRALL SOBY

yves tanguy

The Museum of Modern Art

New York

Copyright 1955 by the Museum of Modern Art, New York

Printed in the United States of America

Library of Congress Catalogue Card Number: 55-11796

contents

LENDERS TO THE EXHIBITION

Mr. and Mrs. LeRay W. Berdeau, Palm Beach; André Breton, Paris; Mme Simone Collinet, Paris; H. Sage Goodwin, Hartford, Conn.; John Goodwin, New York; Claude Hersent, Meudon, France; Ambassador and Mrs. Henri Hoppenot, Saigon, Indo China; Mr. and Mrs. Pierre Matisse, New York; Mr. and Mrs. Millard Meiss, Cambridge, Mass.; Roland Penrose, London; Mrs. Yves Tanguy, Woodbury, Conn.; Mr. and Mrs. Harry L. Winston, Birmingham, Mich.

Albright Art Gallery, Buffalo; The Art Institute of Chicago; Wadsworth Atheneum, Hartford; The Metropolitan Museum of Art, New York; The Museum of Modern Art, New York; The Whitney Museum of American Art, New York; Philadelphia Museum of Art; College of Fine and Applied Arts, University of Illinois, Urbana; Washington University, St. Louis.

Pierre Matisse Gallery, New York.

acknowledgments

In the preparation of this exhibition and catalogue, my greatest debt is to the artist's wife, Kay Sage Tanguy, and to Pierre Matisse, who was not only Tanguy's dealer but a schoolmate and lifelong friend. Both have helped devotedly with the task of assembling pictures and information, as has Patricia Matisse.

I am also deeply indebted to Marcel Duhamel and Marcel Jean of Paris, who have made available their detailed knowledge of the life and career of their late friend. Duhamel's part in encouraging and helping sustain Tanguy during the latter's formative years as an artist, is recorded in the following pages; Marcel Jean has amplified in letters the biographical material about the painter recorded in his fine article for *Les lettres nouvelles* (bibl.16). Mme Simone Collinet very kindly assisted in locating Tanguy paintings in Parisian collections. André Breton, leader of the surrealist movement of whose esthetic or anti-esthetic Tanguy acted as an almost mediumistic interpreter, has shown a profound interest in the exhibition since it was first announced. From London Roland Penrose and E. L. T. Mesens have sent many pertinent facts about the artist and his imagery.

The difficult task of translating some of the French titles of Tanguy's works was entrusted to Robert Goldwater; other translations were made by Kay Sage Tanguy. As Assistant Director of the exhibition, Margaret Miller has shown her usual perceptive efficiency; Frances Pernas has seen the catalogue through the press with care and dispatch.

The Museum is grateful to Man Ray for permission to use as frontispiece in this book his superb photograph of the artist. On behalf of the Trustees of the Museum, I should like to thank the lenders whose generosity has made the exhibition possible.

JAMES THRALL SOBY, *Director of the Exhibition*

Tanguy, at Lac du Bourget near Chemilieu, 1939

yves tanguy

Tanguy was an artist who never tormented his inspiration. A slow, meticulous crafts-man, working in an impeccable studio, he painted only when the spirit moved him — that steadfast, rare, creative spirit which remains a heartening phenomenon in the art of our time. He abhorred schedules and he abhorred stylistic change for its own sake. I remember his speaking with amused distaste of the attempt by a colleague to organize early hours of work for a group of artists, among them Tanguy, gathered at Chemilieu in 1939. He sometimes talked irritatedly of painters who felt obliged to evolve a new approach every few years, as a means of freshening their own and the public's interest in their work. Once he had found his direction — and he found it with startling abruptness — he followed it with devotion and purity, secret in his quest ("Yves behind the bars of his blue eyes," André Breton once wrote of him), and oblivious of the pres-sures of fashion and commerce. As a result, his life work is integral to an extraordinary degree, its discipline a strengthening rather than a constricting force.

Raymond Georges Yves Tanguy was born on January 5, 1900, on the Place de la Concorde in Paris at the Ministry of the Marine where his father, a retired sea captain, was an administrative official. Paradoxically, he was born in a bed that had belonged to Gustave Courbet, whose Realism's dependence on the external world stands in absolute contrast to Tanguy's faith in the hallucinatory objects and scenes of his subconscious mind. Nevertheless, the name "Gustave" had particular meaning for Tanguy, as he used to say, half in jest, writing down with care the anagram on his own name which Breton had invented from the letters G-u-s-t-a-v-e, Y-N-Y. He always remembered that the imagery of two other Gustaves — Moreau and Doré — had fed his macabre imagina-tion in youth.

Tanguy's childhood vacations were spent at his family's house at Locronan in the Finistère province of Brittany, and unquestionably this was the most important forma-tive fact in the evolution of his vision as an artist. Neither in his art nor in conversation did he often refer in specific terms to childhood experience, though once he reluctantly confessed that he remembered three sources of terror in early youth: bullrushes, large beach chairs and the story of Humpty Dumpty. But the Finistère landscape made an immense impression on him. The fields near Locronan are peopled with menhirs and dolmens from prehistoric times and these, subjectively transformed, are frequent prop-

9

THE BOAT. 1926. Collection Paul Garson, Paris

erties in the dream world Tanguy celebrated as an adult painter. Moreover, he never forgot the vast plateaus of the Brittany midland nor the submarine landscape of its rocky shore, where objects float hesitantly in the underwater light, shifting with the depth and tide.

At Locronan in youth Tanguy often watched a local painter named Toché at work. Toché's aim was to capture the atmospheric qualities of landscape at dusk or at night. For the purpose he viewed his subjects through a dark glass which converted their daylight values into those of evening. The parallel with Tanguy's own procedure as an artist is apparent, though his own transforming agent was imaginative rather than mechanical. Tanguy always spoke respectfully of Toché, admiring the latter's courage in setting up his easel on a busy public square, impervious to interruptions by the curious and the idle. Throughout his own career, Tanguy showed a comparable intentness as an artist. His eye stayed on his painting. He seemed totally indifferent to the murmurs around him, whether those of politeness, derision or applause.

In 1918 Tanguy, reminded of family tradition, shipped out as an apprentice officer on cargo boats bound for Africa and South America, an experience obliquely recorded in one of his very early pictures (*above*). In 1920 he was drafted for service in the

10

French Army, and was attached to an infantry regiment stationed at Lunéville. Life in the provincial barracks brought on an acute state of depression. He put an end to his ordeal by volunteering for service in Tunis and was finally released by the Army. But at Lunéville he had met a fellow-Breton, the poet and film director Jacques Prévert, who was to become one of the closest companions of his first years as an artist.

Reunited in Paris in 1922, Tanguy and Prévert somehow kept alive on the scantiest of funds and pondered what careers to follow. Both had strong literary inclinations (throughout his life Tanguy read constantly), and both seem to have been elated by their discovery of the Comte de Lautréamont's book, *Les Chants de Maldoror,* later a central influence on the surrealist movement as a whole. But Tanguy had begun to make sketches on scraps of paper and on the tablecloths and napkins of the Montparnasse cafés. These sketches attracted the attention of Maurice Vlaminck, one of many painters whose connoisseurship may well have been more remarkable than his art, and at this point Tanguy thought of becoming an artist. His mind was made up one day in 1923 when, riding down the rue de La Boétie on a bus, he saw a painting in the window of Paul Guillaume's gallery. The picture was an early work by Giorgio de Chirico, now coupled with Tanguy in the present exhibition. Tanguy was so struck by the picture's enigmatic imagery that he jumped off the bus and ran over to examine it. On that day he determined to be himself a painter. Only some years later did he discover that André Breton, founder of the surrealist movement in which Tanguy's art was to play an important part, had come upon de Chirico's "metaphysical" works in precisely the same way.

Tanguy's progress as an artist was slow at first, the more so in that it never seems to have occurred to him to seek instruction of any kind. But he apparently completed

(Left to right) Tanguy with Marcel Duhamel, Jacques Prévert and Pierre Prévert, at Locronan, Brittany, 1924

11

RUE DE LA SANTÉ. 1925. Collection Marcel Duhamel, Paris

a good number of canvases during the early 1920s. Marcel Duhamel, who had found
a house for Tanguy, Prévert and himself at 54 rue du Chateau, behind the Montparnasse railroad station, remembers Tanguy feeding picture after picture into a
blazing fireplace, in an hour of despair. In any case, few paintings prior to 1926 sur-
vive, and Tanguy almost always dated his works from the very beginning — one more
indication of the methodical turn of mind which underlay his fantasy. Among these
works is a street scene (*above*), whose deep perspective and wry architectural distor-
tions recall Tanguy's admiration for de Chirico's "Italian squares" of the years just
preceding the First World War.

In 1925 Tanguy met André Breton through mutual friends. The previous December
the magazine, *La Révolution Surréaliste,* had been launched, with Pierre Naville and
Benjamin Péret as editors and Breton as guiding force. Tanguy, having seen the magazine, was predisposed to join Breton and the other surrealists; in the issue of June 15,
1926, the magazine published its first reproduction of one of his works, and thereafter
he was recognized as one of the "official" surrealist artists.

Tanguy's paintings of 1926 are admittedly naive in execution. In one of them
(*opposite*), a theatrical performance of levitation takes place against a murky backdrop,

12

spattered by flashes of light. The backdrop would presently be transformed into the dark, far landscape of *The Storm* (page 24), in which lightning flares in a turgid sky. And the very subject of Tanguy's 1926 picture of levitation is pertinent to his later art. In many of his paintings objects float, rise or fall as though by invisible magic. These objects are not believably lighter than air, nor yet much heavier. Often the largest of them skim the ground indecisively, like waterlogged substances refusing — by inches — the ocean floor.

It was in 1927 that Tanguy, with astonishing abruptness, found his way as an artist. Whereas his works reproduced in *La Révolution Surréaliste* for 1926 show the influence of Masson, Ernst and Miró (who was at that time a frequent visitor at 54 rue du Chateau), the following year Tanguy produced a series of thoroughly personal images.

The series begins, perhaps, with *He Did What He Wanted* (page 23), in which the foreground's conical, geometric form, surmounted by lettering, is reminiscent of the cryptic objects in the paintings of de Chirico's Ferrarese period (1915-18), and in which

AT THE FAIR. 1926. Collection Marcel Duhamel, Paris

GENESIS (*Genèse*). 1926. Oil, 39⅜ x 31⅞″. Collection Claude Hersent, Meudon, France

The Storm's human figure with arms encircled by ribbons again makes its appearance. The geometric object shares the foreground with an octopus-like mollusk, hugging the sand and blowing forth its protective ink. The dunes rear sharply upward beyond, and in the distant sky we see one of those lacy, translucent forms which recur often in Tanguy's art; ectoplasmic swirls of color billow in from the right. The *Shadow Country* (page 25) again uses one of Tanguy's favorite compositional formulas — a deep foreground plain bounded in the distance by a narrow band of sky, where objects float mysteriously in the silent air, above the huddled dolmens below.

The three climactic pictures of the 1927 series are: *A Large Picture Which Is a Landscape* (page 31), *The Extinction of Useless Lights* (page 26) and *Mama, Papa Is Wounded!* (page 27), its title taken from a psychiatric case history. The ground in the first-named picture is striated with heavy shadows on which wisps of seaweed grow, and at the left a strange mesa presides over the ominous calm. Tanguy's objects have now tended to congeal into hard kernels, shaped like puffed grains of cereal and casting dense, black shadows. In *The Extinction of Useless Lights,* the landscape seems to be one from which the sea has just receded (and indeed a fish still swims unaware in the sky), and a mysterious monument with outstretched hand guides on a string a passing cloud.

In the famous *Mama, Papa Is Wounded!,* a hairy stalk rises at the right against dark gusts of color, and the illusion of limitless space is heightened by a linear cat's cradle binding the flecked shadows on the earth. The picture illustrates with extraordinary acuteness a relative constant of Tanguy's technique: the dual manipulation of perspective, from far to near and from high to low. Naturally, conventional perspective presupposes both depth and height, but perhaps no other modern painter has so insistently dramatized an opposition between these two dimensions. The fascination of *Mama, Papa* stems in part from its ambiguous placing of forms within vertical space, as when two of the foreground objects (the one at the right resembling a fish with popping eyes) coast in the air above their shadows, as if gravity had lost its hold and released a chimerical medley above the placid earth. Or, as if the entire scene took place in an aquarium mechanically provided with a lighted horizon.

The years 1928 and 1929 were slightly less prolific for the artist, though during them he completed a number of his finest early works, among them *The Mood of Now, Old Horizon* and *The Lovers* (pages 30, 32, 33). All three pictures typify the astonishing technical progress Tanguy had made since 1926. The wind-swept landscape of *The Mood of Now* evokes a supernatural mood, as objects drift in the imponderable haze. The dark *Old Horizon* affirms Tanguy's essential solemnity as a painter — a quality standing in marked contrast to the deliberate playfulness of much surrealist art. In *The Lovers,* with its superbly modeled, air-borne forms, the compositional device of the two pictures just discussed is reversed. Instead of portraying long vistas of land

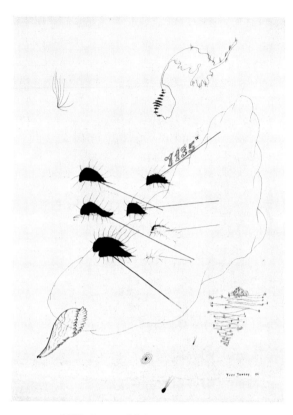

DRAWING. 1926. Pen and ink, 13 x 10". The Museum of
Modern Art, New York

against a far, low sky, the picture becomes virtually a skyscape, bounded in the foreground by a narrow shelf of earth.

In 1930 and 1931, after a trip to Africa, Tanguy completed a series of six or seven
canvases, among them *The Armoire of Proteus* (page 34), which are isolated within his
art as a whole. These images, with their fluted tablelands and jigsaw bastions, differ
sharply from previous and subsequent paintings. Tanguy had been impressed by some
curious rock formations he saw on his travels in Africa (he had been totally indifferent
to exotic local color and the traditional aspects of orientalism), and had been amazed
by the clarity of African sunlight. The rocks he saw seem to have suggested cliff dwell-
ings guarded by unlikely beacons and covered with enigmatic monuments, like nothing
in any known guidebook. He painted them in clear, penetrating light, leaving far
behind the atmospheric murkiness of his earlier works and using vigorously incised
contours.

16

A principal reason for the stylistic change was that the African pictures, unlike all the others in Tanguy's *oeuvre*, were sketched on the canvas before being painted. The artist once told me that on his return from Africa he felt the need of discipline in drawing and in a more fixed placing of forms. But the experiment was short-lived because, as he said, "I found that if I planned a picture beforehand, it never surprised me, and surprises are my pleasure in painting." He added that what interested him most as a painter was the way in which one motif suggested a second, a third, a fourth, unpredictably. Tanguy's spontaneous generation of forms — a chain reaction, as of bundled firecrackers — is well illustrated by *The Ribbon of Extremes* (page 36), in which objects have multiplied astonishingly and are assembled in quiet conclave at the extreme foreground of the canvas, before a broad area of sky.

After his African voyage, Tanguy usually substituted mineral forms for the vegetal

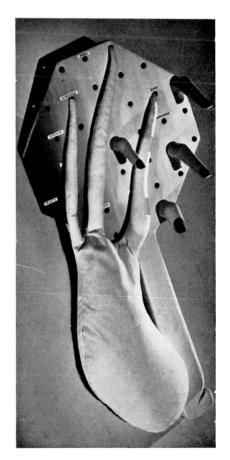

FROM THE OTHER SIDE OF THE BRIDGE (*De l'autre côté du pont*). 1936. Object, 19 x 8¼". Collection Charles Ratton, Paris

ones used in earlier works. His color became more complex and varied, with extremes of light and dark replacing the relatively even tonality of his previous pictures. At the same time he made more and more frequent use of one of his most poetic inventions — the melting of land into sky, one image metamorphosed into another, as in the moving-picture technique known as lap-dissolve. The fixed horizon was now often replaced by a continuous and flowing treatment of space, and in many paintings of the 1930s and 1940s, among them *Movements and Acts* (page 38) and *The Furniture of Time* (page 41), it is extremely difficult to determine at what point earth becomes sky or whether objects rest on the ground or float aloft. The ambiguity is intensified by changes in the density of the objects themselves, from opaque to translucent to transparent, creating a spatial *double entendre.*

Though Tanguy's detractors have sometimes complained of his uniformity, there is in fact a very considerable range of development in his art. How completely different, for example, are the sombre *Movements and Acts* of 1937 and the giddily colorful *Extinction of the Species* (page 40), painted the following year. The scale of Tanguy's forms changes drastically, too, from the fairly minute precision of *The Five Strangers* (page 43) to the bold monumentality of *Slowly Toward the North* (page 44). Within a single year the spindled elements of certain works of 1943 were replaced by the massive, osseous forms of *My Life White and Black* (page 49).

In 1939 Tanguy had come to America and presently he and his wife, the painter Kay Sage, bought an early nineteenth-century farmhouse at Woodbury, Connecticut, where he lived until his sudden, tragic death in January, 1955. Directly behind the house rises a steep, bare hill whose puzzling contours might have been designed by Tanguy himself, since they upset traditional concepts of scale and recall the dazzling inclines sometimes experienced in dreams. His removal to a foreign land caused no fundamental change in Tanguy's art, which always stemmed from inner sources. But in America he tended to become a more audacious colorist and to work occasionally on larger canvases, as in *The Palace of the Windowed Rocks* (page 45), the largest picture he ever painted, perhaps because it was virtually commissioned as a central piece in the exhibition of surrealist art, organized by André Breton and Marcel Duchamp at the Reid mansion on Madison Avenue in 1942.

During the war years Tanguy completed at Woodbury a number of extremely rich and handsome works, among them *Slowly Toward the North,* (page 44) *Wine, Honey and Oil* (page 46) and — perhaps the most memorable of all in poetic quality — *Indefinite Divisibility* (page 47), whose mirroring bowls are like dream-transfigurations of the pie plates in Bruegel's *Country of Cocaigne.* He worked slowly and only when he felt so impelled. His studio in a barn behind the Woodbury house was a spotless white, and near his easel his colors were laid out in a compartmented wooden box he had made with as much skill and care as he lavished on a chess set he carved for his own and his

Chess Set. c. 1950. Carved wood, king 4″ high; board, 21 x 21″. Collection Mrs. Yves Tanguy, Woodbury, Conn.

wife's delectation (*above*). (The set was a replica of a set carved from a broom handle which Tanguy gave to the sculptor, Brancusi, before leaving Paris.)

Neatness and precision were deeply ingrained attributes of Tanguy's mind and personality. He loved objects that were beautifully made, as one could not fail to realize when he displayed his collection of guns, with telescopic sights finely mounted by a neighboring gunsmith. Tanguy talked eloquently and with care and humor; his manner was almost courtly at times, though never in any sense pretentious. These may seem odd facts to record, considering Tanguy's position as a leading artist of the surrealist movement, whose adherents often stressed a new kind of poetic license and despised convention's strictures. But they help explain Tanguy's unique achievement as a profound craftsman and an easel painter in the classical sense of the term. His subconscious visions were never scribbled, as in the "automatic" images of some of his colleagues, but were communicated with the utmost finesse. He was justified in saying once: "I expect nothing from my reflections, but I am sure of my reflexes."

Toward the end of the Second World War, Tanguy's reflexes functioned with particular certainty, as he completed such works as *The Closing Days; Closed Sea, Wide World; The Rapidity of Sleep* and the magic little *The Sifter of Gold* (pages 48, 51, 52, 53), which recaptures the romantic ambience of his works of 1927-29. In this country white and gray became favorite colors, and were used to bind and oppose his stronger hues — "nasturtium, *coq de roche*, poplar leaf, rusty well-chain, cut sodium, slate, jellyfish and cinnamon," as Breton once defined them. *Suffering Softens Stones; The Transparent Ones* (pages 56, 59) typify the postwar series, and in such works as *Fear* (page 63)

Frederick Sommer: CACTUS AND ROCKS. 1943. The Museum of Modern Art, Photography Collection

he used intricate stalactite borders at one or both of the vertical edges of his composi-
tions, framing wispy skies. Perhaps at this point, more than ever, he deserved to be
called a painters' painter. At least artists of quite opposite tendency have marveled at
his technical skill and sensitivity. He remained faithful to surrealism's basic tenets,
but sometimes, watching him hold his volume of Montaigne's essays and hearing him
say of it "everything is here," one knew that he was the spiritual heir of Chardin no less
than of Isidore Ducasse, the so-called "Comte de Lautréamont."

In the right foreground section of *Rose of the Four Winds* (page 58) there occurs,
perhaps for the first time, that breathless congestion of boulders, pebbles or bones which
will reach its brilliant climax in *Multiplication of the Arcs* (page 67). Could it be
possible that Tanguy had stored away somewhere in memory the rocky landscape with
giant cacti in Arizona, as recorded by a photographer-friend, Frederick Sommer (*above*)?

Tanguy himself never saw this particular landscape, but he did see parts of Arizona and, like his colleague, Max Ernst, was startled by the geological phenomena of the American West, which both visited soon after their arrival here in 1939. At any rate, *Rose of the Four Winds* suggests the Western wastelands, and Tanguy may well have kept them in mind until finally, through that slow alchemy which characterized his imaginative process, they found their place in his art. *The Hunted Sky* (page 60), also painted in 1951, assembles stony forms in mannequin-like piles, their relative uniformity of coloring relieved by stark white objects, like bits of paper blowing or settling in the arid, desert air.

During 1952 and 1953 Tanguy produced a marvelous series of drawings (pages 61, 62, 65) but few paintings, in part because of ill health, in part because he and his wife traveled abroad to attend the openings of their solo exhibitions in Paris and Rome (Tanguy also showed his pictures in Milan). But back in Woodbury, to his vast relief, he began to work again, painting the fine *The Mirage of Time* (page 64) and the two sparkling little canvases, *Saltimbanques* and *Where Are You?* (page 66). And during the final months of his life he completed what is almost certainly the greatest work of his entire, dedicated career — *Multiplication of the Arcs.*

Tanguy, at Woodbury, Connecticut

I saw Tanguy several times in Woodbury when the *Multiplication* was in progress. He worked on the picture like one possessed, hurrying back to his studio after a brief lunch, whereas ordinarily he would have sat for hours, talking about literature and pictures (though never about his own, unless stubbornly pressed) and the state of the world of art, with its chronic feuds and armistices, its developments and counter-developments. Clearly he sensed that the *Multiplication* was to be the summary of lifelong aims and preoccupations; he would arrive at the house at the end of the day exhausted by the long hours of unrelenting concentration. And what a cosmic image he achieved! The picture is a sort of boneyard of the world, its inexplicable objects gathered in fantastic profusion before a soft and brooding sky. The close gradations of light, tone and form are handled with such acumen that a pristine order evolves, whose poetic impact is more than likely to establish the picture as one of the masterworks in the art of our time.

THE GIRL WITH RED HAIR (*La Fille aux cheveux rouges*). 1926. Oil on canvas, 24 x 18¼". Collection Mr. and Mrs. Pierre Matisse, New York

HE DID WHAT HE WANTED (*Il faisait ce qu'il voulait*). 1927. Oil on canvas, 31⅞ x 25⅝". Collection André Breton, Paris

THE STORM (*L'Orage*). 1926. Oil on canvas, 32 x 25¾". Philadelphia Museum of Art, The Louise and Walter Arensberg Collection

SHADOW COUNTRY (*Terre d'ombre*). 1927. Oil on canvas, 39 x 31⅝". Collection Mr. and Mrs. Harry L. Winston, Birmingham, Michigan

EXTINCTION OF USELESS LIGHTS (*L'Extinction des lumières inutiles*). 1927. Oil on canvas, 36¼ x 25¾". The Museum of Modern Art, New York

MAMA, PAPA IS WOUNDED! (*Mama, Papa est blessé!*). 1927. Oil on canvas, 36¼ x 28¾". The Museum of Modern Art, New York

WHEN THEY SHOOT ME (*Quand on me fusillera*). 1927. Oil on wood, 24 x 18⅞".
Collection Mme Simone Collinet, Paris

opposite: WITH MY SHADOW (*Avec mon ombre*). 1928. Oil on canvas, 45⅛ x 32⅛". Collection
Mrs. Pierre Matisse, New York.

THE MOOD OF NOW (*L'Humeur des temps*). 1928. Oil on canvas, 36¼ x 28¾". Collection Mme Simone Collinet, Paris

opposite: A LARGE PICTURE WHICH IS A LANDSCAPE (*Un Grand tableau qui représente un paysage*). 1927. Oil on canvas, 46 x 35¾". Collection Ambassador and Mrs. Henri Hoppenot, Saigon, Indo-China

OLD HORIZON (*Vieil horizon*). 1928. Oil on canvas, 39⅜ x 28⅞". Pierre Matisse Gallery, New York

THE LOVERS (*Les Amoureux*). 1929. Oil on canvas, 39⅜ x 32". Private collection, New York

THE ARMOIRE OF PROTEUS (*L'Armoire de Protée*). 1931. Oil on canvas, 24 x 19¾". Collection André Breton, Paris

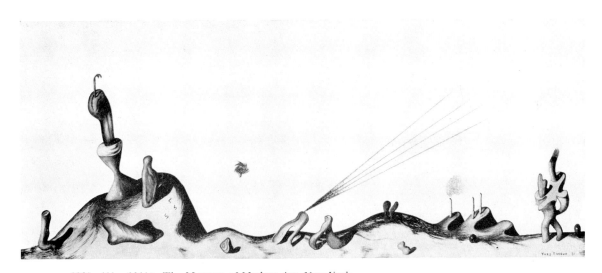

GOUACHE. 1931. 4½ x 11½". The Museum of Modern Art, New York

THE RIBBON OF EXTREMES (*Le Ruban des excès*). 1932. Oil on wood, 13¾ x 17¾". Collection Roland Penrose, London

A RISK IN EACH HAND (*Un Risque dans chaque main*). 1934. Oil on canvas, 25¼ x 21⅛".
Collection John Goodwin, New York

MOVEMENTS AND ACTS (*Les Mouvements et les actes*). 1937. Oil on canvas, 25½ x 20¾". Collection Mrs. Yves Tanguy, Woodbury, Conn.

THE DOUBTER (*Le Questionnant*). 1937. Oil, 23¾ x 31⅞". Collection Roland Penrose, London

EXTINCTION OF THE SPECIES (*L'Extinction des espèces*). 1938. Oil on canvas, 36⅛ x 28¾″. Pierre Matisse Gallery, New York

opposite: THE FURNITURE OF TIME (*Le Temps meublé*). 1939. Oil on canvas. 45⅞ x 35⅛″. Private collection

THE WITNESS (*Le Temoin*). 1940. Oil on canvas, 36 x 28″. Collection Mr. and Mrs. LeRay W. Berdeau, Palm Beach

THE FIVE STRANGERS (*Les Cinq étrangers*). 1941. Oil on canvas, 38⅝ x 32". Wadsworth Atheneum, Hartford

SLOWLY TOWARD THE NORTH (*Vers le nord lentement*). 1942. Oil on canvas, 42 x 36″. The Museum of Modern Art, New York gift of Philip C. Johnson

opposite: THE PALACE OF THE WINDOWED ROCKS (*Le Palais aux rochers de fenêtres*). 1942. Oil on canvas, 64 x 52″. Collection Pierre Matisse, New York

WINE, HONEY AND OIL (*Vin, miel et huile*). 1942. Oil on canvas, 20 x 30″. Collection Mr. and Mrs. Millard Meiss, Cambridge, Mass.

opposite: INDEFINITE DIVISIBILITY (*Divisibilité indéfinie*). 1942. Oil on canvas, 40 x 35″. Room of Contemporary Art Collection, Albright Art Gallery, Buffalo

THE CLOSING DAYS (*Les Derniers jours*). 1944. Oil on Canvas, 38¼ x 54⅛″. Pierre Matisse Gallery, New York

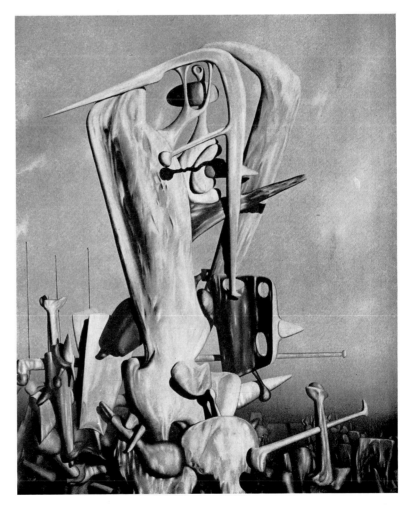

MY LIFE WHITE AND BLACK (*Ma vie blanche et noire*). 1944. Oil on canvas, 36 x 30″. Pierre Matisse Gallery, New York

TOWER OF THE SEA (*La Tour marine*). 1944.
Oil on canvas, 36 x 13¾". Washington University, St. Louis

CLOSED SEA, WIDE WORLD (*Mer close, monde ouvert*). 1944. Oil on canvas, 23 x 50″. Pierre Matisse Gallery, New York

52

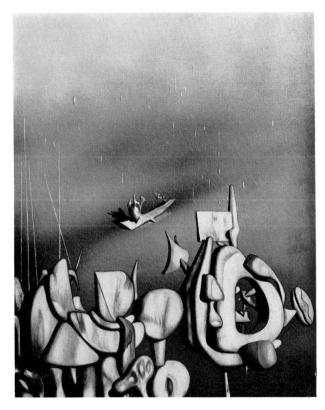

THE SIFTER OF GOLD (*L'Orpailleuse*). 1945. Oil on canvas, 18 x 15⅛″. Pierre Matisse Gallery, New York

opposite: THE RAPIDITY OF SLEEP (*La Rapidité de sommeil*). 1945. Oil on canvas, 50 x 40″. The Art Institute of Chicago, Joseph Winterbotham Collection

CONVERSATION (*Les Causeurs*). 1945. Gouache, 14⅛ x 11". Collection Mrs. Yves Tanguy, Woodbury, Conn.

54

LADY OF ELEVEN (*La Dame de onze heures*). 1947. Gouache, 23½ x 17½". Pierre Matisse Gallery, New York

SUFFERING SOFTENS STONES (*Le Malheur adoucit les pierres*). 1948. Oil on canvas, 36 x 28″. College of Fine and Applied Arts, University of Illinois, Urbana

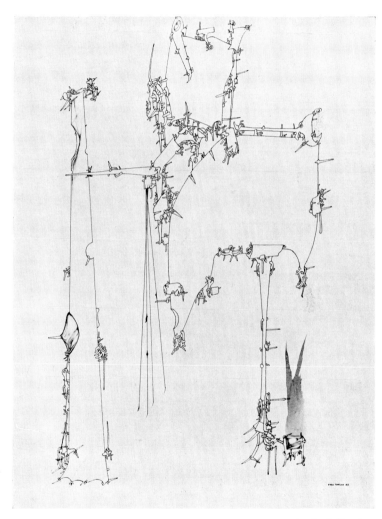

Drawing. 1949. Pen and pencil with watercolor, 19⅞ x 14¾". Collection
Mrs. Yves Tanguy, Woodbury, Conn.

ROSE OF THE FOUR WINDS (*La Rose des quatre vents*). 1950. Oil on canvas, 28 x 23″.
Pierre Matisse Gallery, New York

THE TRANSPARENT ONES (*Les Transparents*). 1951. Oil on canvas, 39 x 32″. Pierre Matisse Gallery, New York

THE HUNTED SKY (*Le Ciel traqué*). 1951. Oil on canvas, 39 x 32″. Collection Mrs. Yves Tanguy, Woodbury. Conn.

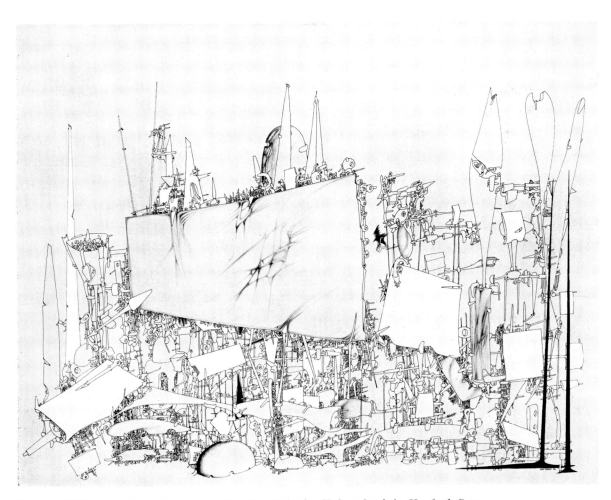

Drawing. 1952. Pen and ink with gouache, 27 x 22″. Collection H. Sage Goodwin, Hartford, Conn.

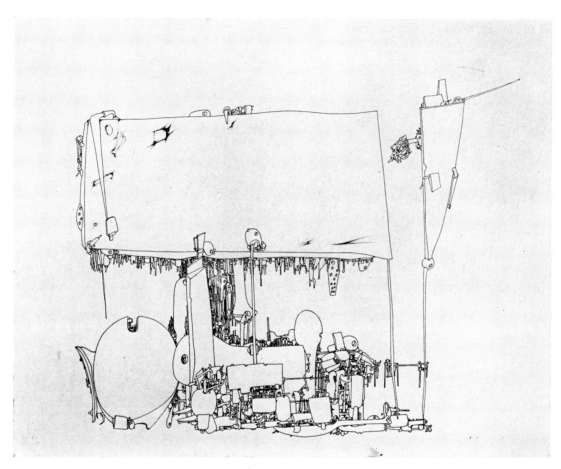

Drawing. 1953. Ink and pencil, 22¼ x 28⅛". Collection Mrs. Yves Tanguy, Woodbury, Conn.

opposite: FEAR (*La Peur*). 1949. Oil on canvas, 60⅛ x 40". Whitney Museum of American Art, New York

THE MIRAGE OF TIME (*Mirage le temps*). 1954. Oil on canvas, 39 x 32″. The Metropolitan Museum of Art, New York

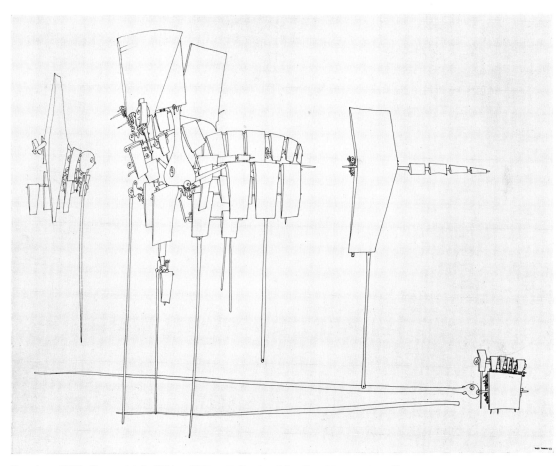

Drawing. 1953. Pen and ink, 22¼ x 28⅛″. Collection Mrs. Yves Tanguy, Woodbury, Conn.

SALTIMBANQUES (*Les Saltimbanques*). 1954. Oil on canvas, 17 x 13″. Collection Mrs. Yves Tanguy, Woodbury, Conn.

WHERE ARE YOU? (*Où es tu?*). 1954. Oil on canvas, 10⅛ x 7⅞″. Collection Mrs. Yves Tanguy, Woodbury, Conn.

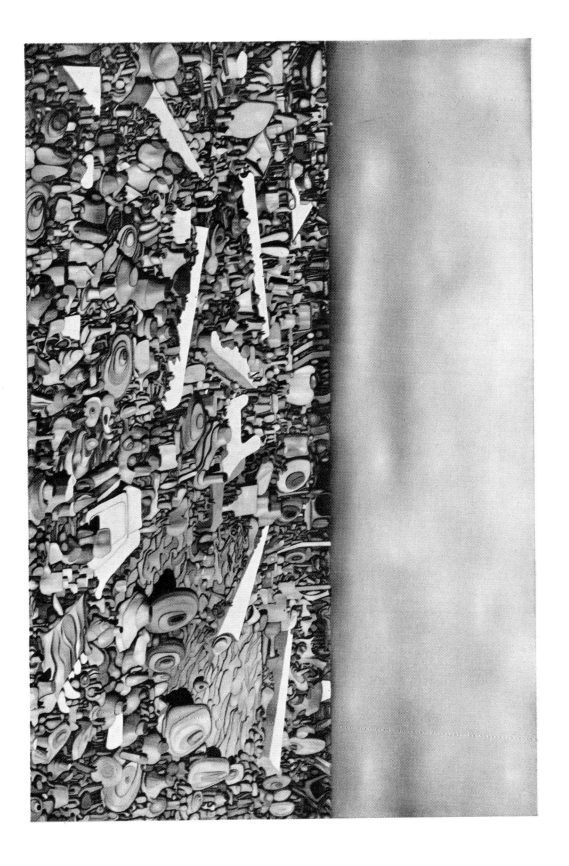

MULTIPLICATION OF THE ARTS (*Multiplication des arts*). 1954. Oil on canvas, 40 x 60". The Museum of Modern Art, New York. Mrs. Simon Guggenheim Fund

1 BORISOFF, PAUL. Man is the witness. *Tiger's Eye (N.Y.)* no.7:77-79 ill. Mar. 1949.

2 BRETON, ANDRÉ. Des tendances les plus récentes de la peinture surréaliste. *Minotaure 3 no.12-13: 16-17 May 1939. Partly quoted bibl.14.*

3 BRETON, ANDRÉ. Entretiens, 1913-1952. p.94, 135, 142-3, 152, 179, 242-3, 287   Paris, Gallimard, 1952.

4 BRETON, ANDRÉ. Le Surréalisme et la peinture. 72p. plus 77 ill. Paris, Gallimard, 1928. *Enlarged edition, 1945.*

5 BRETON, ANDRÉ. Le Surréalisme et la peinture, suivi de Genèse et perspective artistiques du surréalisme, et de Fragments inédits. p.173-177 ill. New York, Brentano's, 1945. *"Yves Tanguy" incorporated into bibl.6, 46. "Genèse" translated in bibl.14.*

6 BRETON, ANDRÉ. Yves Tanguy. English translation by Bravig Imbs. 94p. ill. New York, Pierre Matisse, 1946. *French and English text.*

7 CALAS, NICOLAS. Alone. p.189-191 in Comfort, A. & Bayliss, J. New Road 1943. Billericay, Essex, Grey Walls Press, 1943. *Also in bibl.38.*

8 CALAS, NICOLAS. Magic icons. *Horizon 14 no.83:304-315 ill. Nov.1946. On painting by Ernst, Lam, Tanguy, etc.* Also note bibl.43b.

9 ELUARD, PAUL. Donner à voir. p.190-191   Paris, Gallimard, 1939. *Reprinted from "La Vie immédiate" (1932).*

10 ELUARD, PAUL. Voir: poèmes, peintures, dessins. p.59-61 ill. Genève — Paris, Trois Collines, 1948. *Also in bibl.20.*

11 FORD, CHARLES H. Poems for painters. p.[9-10] ill. New York, View, 1945. *Also in bibl.38.*

12 GAFFÉ, RENÉ. Peinture à travers dada et le surréalisme. p.60-62 ill. Bruxelles, Éditions de Artistes, 1952.

13 GASCOYNE, DAVID. Short survey of surrealism. 162p. ill. [London] Cobden-Sanderson, 1935. *Compact account of personalities and the movement from the literary viewpoint.*

14 GUGGENHEIM, PEGGY, ed. Art of this century . . . 1910 to 1942. p.22, 115-117 ill. New York, Art of this century, 1942. *Collection catalog also includes "Genesis and perspective of surrealism" from bibl.5.*

15 HUYGHE, RENÉ. Histoire de l'art contemporain: la peinture. p.337-344 Paris, Alcan, 1935. *Text by Cassou and Bazin. Biographical and bibliographical note originally published in "L'Amour de l'Art," Mar. 1934.*

16 JEAN, MARCEL. Yves Tanguy. *Les Lettres Nouvelles 3 no.25: 367-379 ill. Mar. 1955.*

17 JOUFFROY, ALAIN. Le voyage imaginaire d'Yves Tanguy. *Arts (Paris) no.500:12 ill. Jan.26-Feb.1 1955. Also "Hommage à Yves Tanguy," no.521:11 June 22-28 1955.*

18 LEVY, JULIEN. Surrealism. p.19, 22-23, 31, 150-151 ill. New York, Black Sun, 1936.

19 LEVY, JULIEN. Tanguy, Connecticut sage. *Art News 53 no.5: 24-27 ill. 1954.*

20 LONDON BULLETIN. no.4-5: 32-38 ill. July 1938. *Includes "Yves Tanguy" by A. Breton. — "In the margin of crosswords" by Y. Tanguy (drawings). — Translation of poem by P. Eluard. — Yves Tanguy catalog of show at Guggenheim Jeune. — Biographical notes.*

21 MELVILLE, ROBERT. The snake on the dining room table. *View 6 no.3:9-10 ill. May 1946.*

22 MEZCI, ARPAD. Yves Tanguy. *Les Deux Soeurs no.3: 102-107 ill. May 1947.*

23 NADEAU, MAURICE. Histoire du surréalisme. Paris, Éditions du Seuil, 1945-48. *Vol.1; Histoire. — 2: Documents. Includes texts in which Tanguy participated as signatory.*

24 PÉRET, BENJAMIN. Yves Tanguy, ou L'anatife torpille les Jivaros. *Cahiers d'Art 10 no.5-6: 108-110 ill. 1935. Translation in bibl.38.*

25 RAYNAL, MAURICE. Modern painting. p.249, 319 ill. Geneva, Skira, 1953. *Biographical note and bibliography also noted in: History of modern painting, [v.3]: From Picasso to Surrealism (1950). Documentation reprinted bibl.46 and elsewhere.*

26 READ, HERBERT, ed. Surrealism. 251p. New York, Harcourt, Brace [1936]. *Illustrations.*

27 RENNE, RENÉ & SERBANNE, CLAUDE. Yves Tanguy, or The mirror of wonders. *View* 5 no.5: 13-14, 16 ill. Dec. 1945.

28 LA RÉVOLUTION SURRÉALISTE. no.1-12 Dec.1924-Dec.1929. *Reproductions of Tanguy's early work brought the artist to public attention.*

29 SOBY, JAMES T. After Picasso. p.103-104 ill. Hartford, Mitchell; New York, Dodd, Mead, 1935.

30 SOBY, JAMES T. Double solitaire. *Saturday Review of Literature* 37:29-30 ill. Sept. 4 1954. *Retrospective exhibition at the Wadsworth Atheneum.*

31 SOBY, JAMES T. The early Chirico. p.95-97 New York, Dodd Mead, 1941.

32 SOBY, JAMES T. Inland in the subconscious. *Magazine of Art* 42:2-7 ill. Jan.1949.

32aSWEENEY, J. J. See bibl. 35, 38, 43.

33 SYLVESTER, DAVID. Yves Tanguy. *Art News and Review* 2 no.9:5-6 June 3 1950.

34 TANGUY, YVES. In the margin of cross-words. *London Bulletin* no.4-5:33-35 ill. July 1938.

35 TANGUY, YVES. [Interview]. *Museum of Modern Art Bulletin* 13 no.4-5:22-23 ill. Sept.1946. *Interview by J. J. Sweeney in "Eleven Europeans in America" number. List of exhibitions, 1939-45.*

36 TANGUY, YVES. Poids et couleurs. *Le Surréalisme au Service de la Révolution* no.3:27 ill. Dec.1931. *Other numbers contain occasional illustrations and comments, e.g. no.6, 1933.*

37 TYLER, PARKER. Stettheimer, Frances, Leonid, Tanguy. *View* 7 no.2: 36-39 ill. Dec.1936. *Exhibition reviews.*

38 VIEW MAGAZINE. Tanguy. [24]p. ill. New York, 1942. *Special double-number:Tanguy — Tchelitchew, 2nd series, no. 2, May 1942. Includes catalog of Matisse Gallery show (Apr.21-May 9); "What Tanguy veils and reveals" (from bibl.5); "Alone" (from bibl.7); "Tanguy" (from bibl.24); poem by Ford (bibl.11); J. J. Sweeney's "Iconographer of melancholy"; lists of illustrated books and texts, private collections and exhibitions.*

39 WYSS, DIETER. Der Surrealismus. p.83 ill. Heidelberg, Schneider, 1950.

SELECTED CATALOGS

40 BASEL. KUNSTHALLE. Phantastische Kunst des XX. Jahrhunderts. 1952. *Held Aug.30-Oct.12; illustrated; no.211-225 by Tanguy.*

41 BRUSSELS. PALAIS DES BEAUX-ARTS. E.L.T. Mesens présente trois peintres surréalistes: René Magritte, Man Ray, Yves Tanguy. 1937. *Held Dec. 11-22; illustrated; no.59-76 and addenda by Tanguy. Preface by Jean Scutenaire; poem by Eluard.*

41aLONDON. GUGGENHEIM JEUNE. Yves Tanguy.1938. *Held July 1938. 25 works and addenda by Tanguy; see London Bulletin, bibl.20.*

42 NEW YORK. MUSEUM OF MODERN ART. Fantastic art, dada, surrealism. Edited by A.H. Barr, Jr.; essays by G. Hugnet. 1936. *Held Dec. 7, 1936-Jan. 17, 1937; illustrated; no.498-510 by Tanguy; notes.*

43 NEW YORK. PIERRE MATISSE GALLERY. Yves Tanguy. 1939. *Held Dec.12-30; 30 works; preface by J. J. Sweeney.*

43aNEW YORK. PIERRE MATISSE GALLERY. Yves Tanguy. 1942. *Held Apr.21-May 9; illustrated; 14 works. See bibl.38.*

43bNEW YORK. PIERRE MATISSE GALLERY. Yves Tanguy. 1950. *Held Apr.4-22; 18 paintings 2 gouaches, drawings; preface by N. Calas.*

44 PARIS. EXPOSITION INTERNATIONALE DU SURRÉALISME. Le Surrealisme en 1947, présentée par André Breton et Marcel Duchamp. Paris, Galerie Maeght, 1947. *Held July-Aug.; illustrated; additional illustrations in edition de luxe.*

44a PARIS. GALERIE JEANNE BUCHER-MYRBOR. Exposition Yves Tanguy. 1938. *Held May 17-30; prologue by A. Breton.*

45 PARIS. SURRÉALISTE GALERIE. Yves Tanguy & objets d'Amérique. 1927. *Held May 27-June 15; illustrated; preface by A. Breton.*

46 ROME. GALLERIA DELL'OBELISCO. Yves Tanguy. 1953. *Held Feb.16; illustrated; 25 works; preface by Breton (bibl.5); notes from Raynal (bibl.25).*

47 WADSWORTH ATHENEUM. Yves Tanguy, Kay Sage. Hartford, Conn., 1954. *Held Aug.10-Sept.28; illustrated; 38 works. Preface by C. E. Buckley; additional notes in Atheneum Bulletin no.49:4 May 1954. Reviewed in bibl.30.*

index to the exhibition

Loans are listed alphabetically by title in both French and English versions

Works illustrated on pages 10, 12, 13, 16, and 17 are not in the exhibition.

IN THE EXHIBITION BUT NOT ILLUSTRATED

GOUACHE. 1947
13⅛ x 9½"
Private collection

COLLAGE DRAWING. 1949
Ink, pencil, pasted paper, 19⅞ x 14¾"
Pierre Matisse Gallery, New York

DRAWING. 1950
Ink, pencil and watercolor, 19⅞ x 14¾"
Pierre Matisse Gallery, New York

THE IMMENSE WINDOW (*La Grande fenêtre*). 1950
Gouache, 25⅝ x 19⅝"
Collection Mrs. Yves Tanguy, Woodbury, Conn.

This book has been printed in August, 1955, for the
Trustees of the Museum of Modern Art
by The John B. Watkins Company, New York